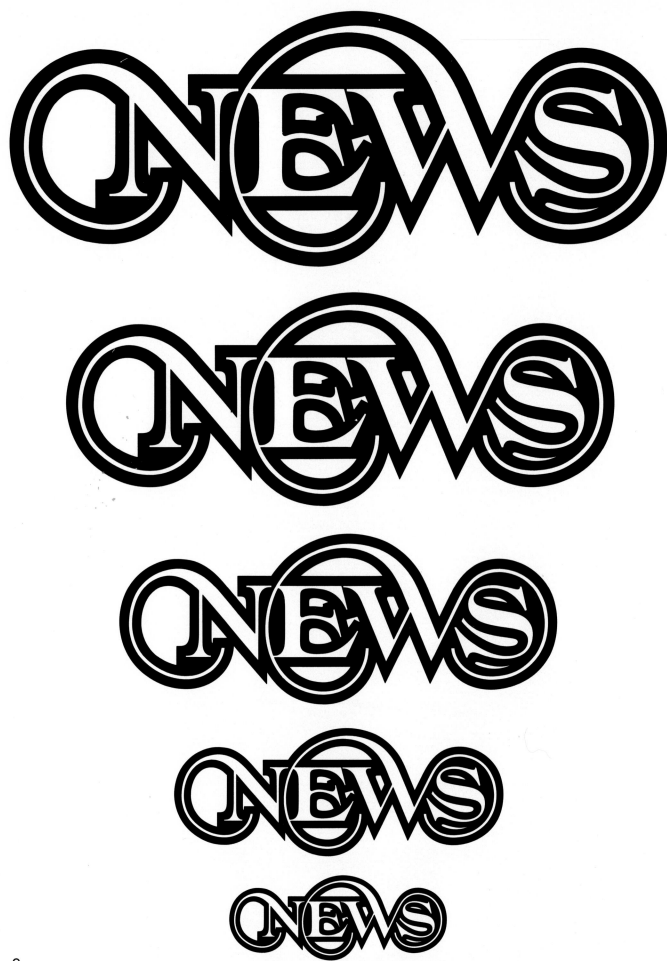

3

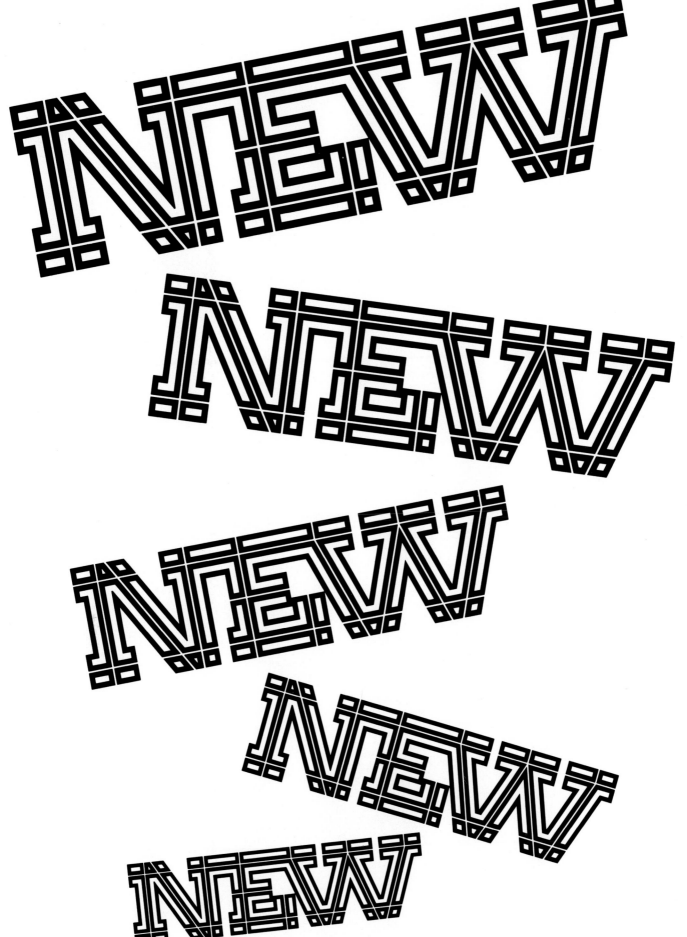

5

Introducing

Introducing

Introducing

Introducing

Introducing

Introducing

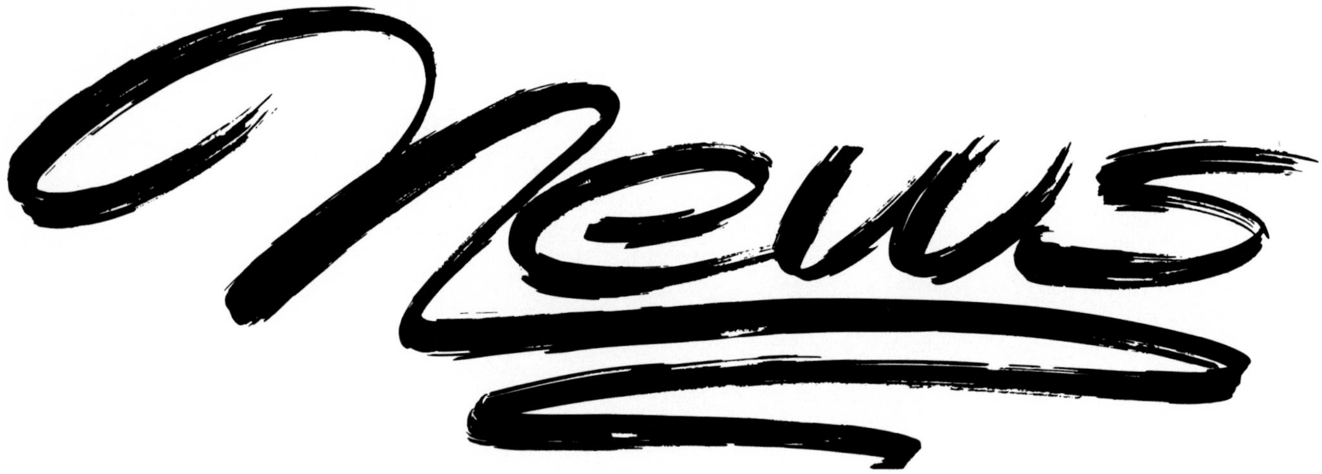
News

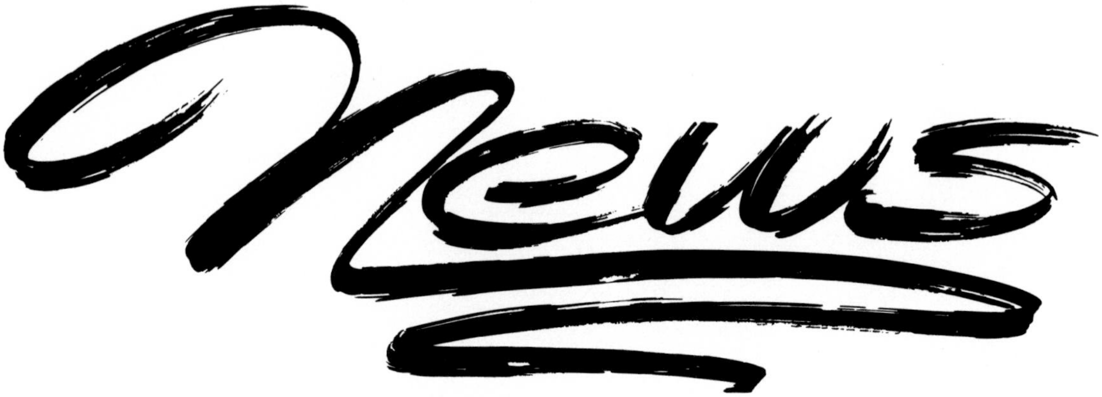
News

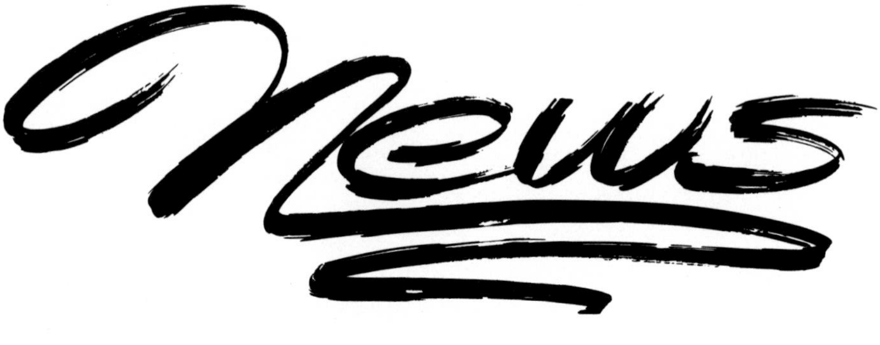
News

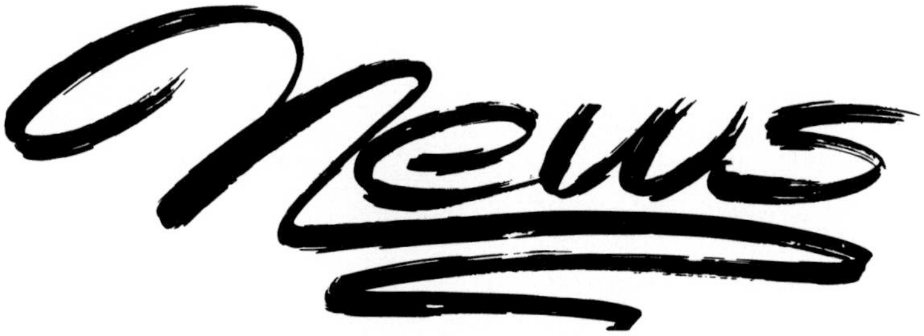
News

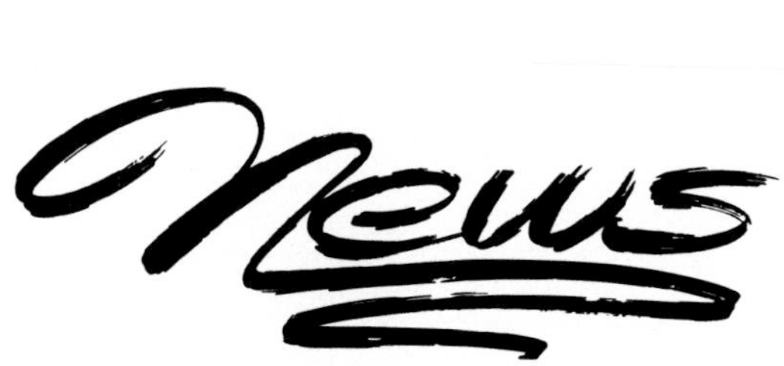
News

ANNOUNCING

ANNOUNCING

ANNOUNCING

ANNOUNCING

Introducing

Introducing

Introducing

NEWS
NEWS
NEWS
NEWS
NEWS
NEWS
NEWS

INTRODUCING

INTRODUCING

INTRODUCING

INTRODUCING

ANNOUNCING

ANNOUNCING

17

ANNOUNCING
ANNOUNCING
ANNOUNCING
ANNOUNCING

NEWS
NEWS
NEWS

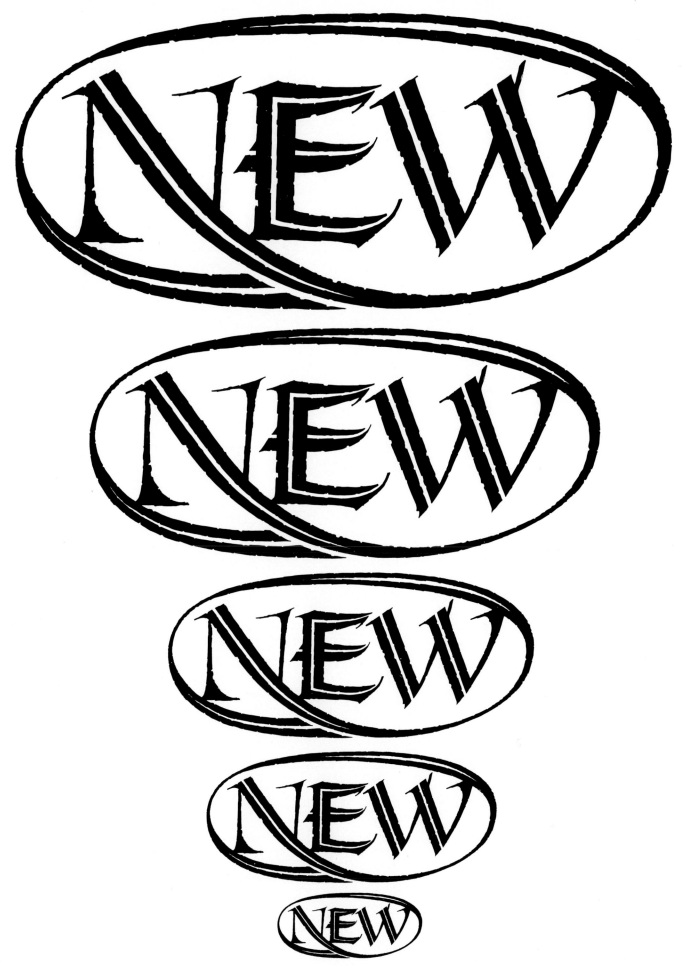

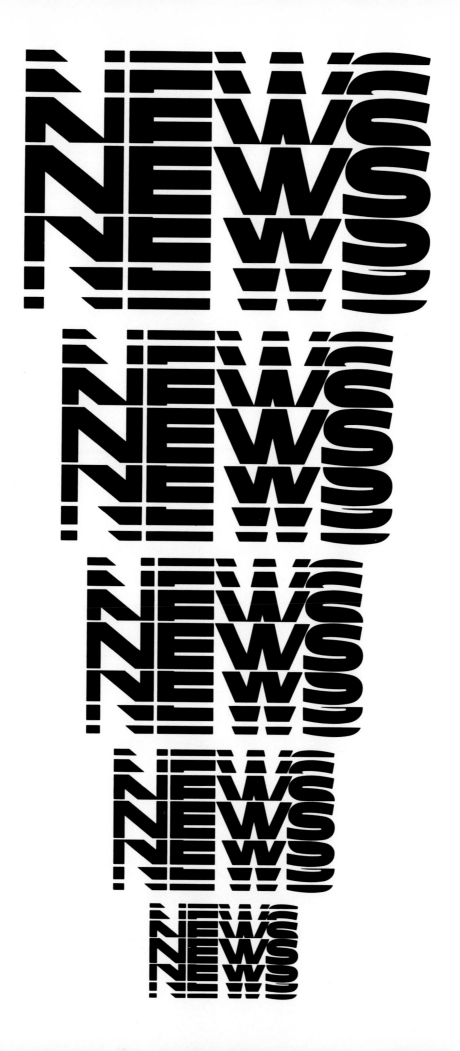

Announcing

Announcing

Announcing

Announcing

Announcing

INTRODUCING

INTRODUCING

INTRODUCING

NEWS

NEWS

NEWS

NEWS

NEWS

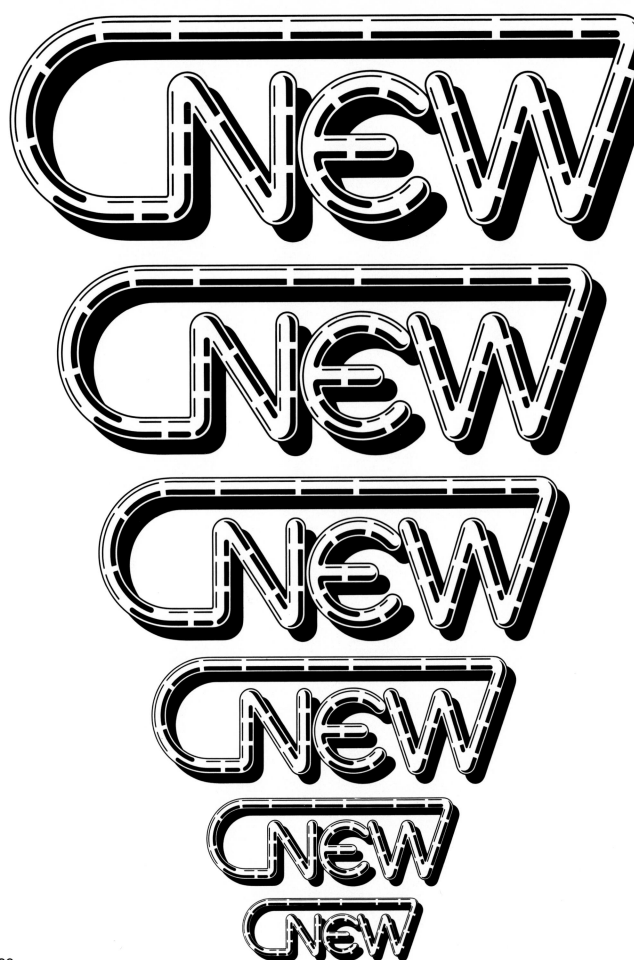

31